(un)Lucky Thirteen
Overcoming Fear, Superstition and Bad Luck

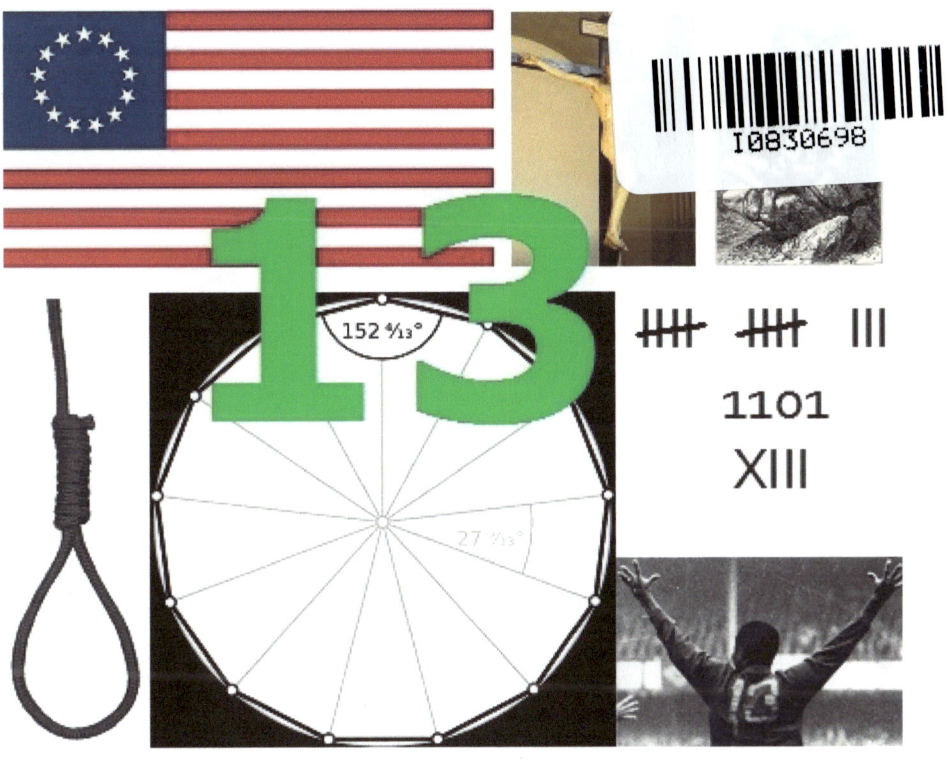

By Gary "Two Horse" Green
& Aaron Brachfeld

VOLUME 7 of the TWO HORSES series

ISBN-13: 978-1721084661

ISBN-10: 1721084665

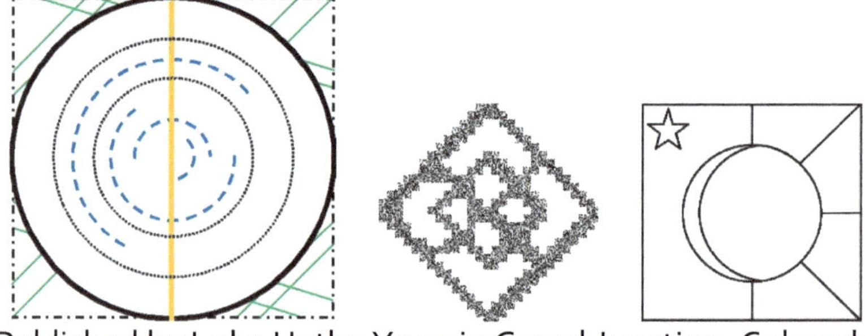

Published by Loka Hatha Yoga in Grand Junction, Colorado

There are many suitable places for your meditation.
We hope this becomes one of them.
Anguttara Nikaya 1.159

LOKAHATHAYOGA@GMAIL.COM - (970) 778-2835
lokahathayoga.blogspot.com

Dedication of Gary Two Horses Green

For and in the Memory of Margaret Moran Green

"Long ago, it must be, I had a photograph. Preserve your memory – it's all that's left me. As I watch the drops of rain, weave their weary paths and lines, I know that I am like the rain. There before the grace of you go I"
-Simon and Garfunkel

"Everytime I see your face, it reminds me of the places we used to go. But all I've got is a photograph and I realize you're not coming back anymore"
-Ringo Starr

ABOUT THE AUTHOR

Gary Two Horse Green is a father and veteran of the Marine Corps where he served as Radio Operator (Crypto), Truck Driver, Forward Observer, NBC (Nuclear, Biological, Chemical) Team Leader. This prepared him to become the proud owner of both dogs and cats.

He is the most interesting man in Virginia: besides working with the USDOT/FRA as a diesel mechanic, Gary has been an on-air personality at both WBEY and WVBK FM, was both DJ and manager of a saloon, and the captain of a racing sailboat. He has lived in 48 states, 8 countries – including Spain and Cuba. He speaks Pirate fluently.

He presently farms in Fairfield, Virginia, programs his friends' computers for free, and contributes to the Loka Review.

TABLE OF CONTENTS

Triskaidekaphobia
Mysterious origins

For as long as anyone can remember, 13, and especially a Friday whose day of the month is 13th, has been considered unlucky, even evil. The fear of 13 has become embedded in our culture and history: many tales and legends have surrounded and reinforced this belief. Hopefully, we don't get hit by lightning talking about it!

<u>Editor's reference file: Triskaidekaphobia</u>
    The fear of 13 (triskaidekaphobia) is ancient, its origination is unknown. However, it is recognized as a kind of disease, a psychological disorder and was "discovered" (defined) by medical science in 1910 when Dr. Isador Henry Coriat, an American Psychologist, published a description of it in his work, "Abnormal Psychology."
    In many cultures, some numbers are irrationally believed to be lucky or unlucky: for some, the number 4, the number 666, the Roman number XVII, (or various other numbers) can illicit as much horror as the number 13. Some days of the week are seen as unlucky, such as Friday.
    There also exists a cultural phenomenon of Triskaidekaphobia manifesting in "missing" floors and terminals and seats (skipping the number 13 between 12 and 14), among other missing 13's, in an either misguided effort to alleviate the fears of Triskaidekaphobiacs, or by an expression of the architect's own Triskaidekaphobia: but respecting the fears of those who suffer from Triskaidekophobia does nothing to alleviate the disease.

Unlucky seat
Ragnarok

In the primitive European cultures, there was a story of how 12 Norse Gods held a banquet: lo and behold, Loki showed up! Loki was not invited to the banquet but when he joined it, his arrival made the gathering 13 in number. Loki, in turn, then killed another banqueter God, and this resulted in the apocalyptic Ragnarok: the deaths of the Gods, numerous natural disasters and the biggest destruction ever seen. According to the story, only two humans survived!

Sound familiar? Guess who else had 12 guests and an uninvited person showed up?

Loki was often an ingenious friend and helper to others, as much as a troublemaker: he is credited with having invented the net

Loki is remembered for his dinnertime dispute with Odin:

"Do you remember, Odin, when in bygone days
we mixed our blood together?
You said you would never drink ale
unless it were brought to both of us"

The Last Supper

If Ragnarok sounds familiar, you might be reminded of the Last Supper. Jesus had all 12 of his disciples gathered together when an uninvited guest showed up. None other than Judas!

<u>**Editor's reference file: Biblical Triskaidekaphobia**</u>
In the Bible, 13 is equally associated with both good and lucky events, as well as bad and unlucky events. However, beginning in the late 19th Century, Christian Triskaidekophiacs increasingly began to use religious reasoning to ground their irrational fears.

Nevertheless, some Christians believe that Jesus was crucified on the 13th – even though the date was more likely April 3rd, 33 AD. And many Christians believe that the whole Cain and Abel debacle happened on the same day Jesus was killed – the 13th of the month, even Friday the 13th!

A coven of witches was believed to be 13 in number by Christians afraid of witchcraft.

The Missing Law

It is sometimes believed that the Babylonians were afraid of the number 13 too: one of the earliest English translations of the Babylonian Code of Hammurabi (originally written 1780 BC) omitted the 13th law.

But in fact the translation by LW King (1910) and edited by Richard Hooker omitted the 13th law because they were themselves afraid of the number 13. Subsequent translations include the "missing law."

And even then, the original did not have any numbering system to the laws! There never was a 13th law of Hammurabi!

Yet in case you were wondering what the omitted law was: "if a seller (in a lawsuit) dies (to evade the contract), the purchaser shall recover damages in the case fivefold from the estate of the seller."

Hammurabi is celebrated in the US Capitol building as one of the greater lawmakers of history

Did you count the steps?

It's the Thought that Counts

Though great lengths are gone to so that those suffering from Triskaidekaphobia are more comfortable (such as skipping the number 13 in floors, terminals, seats, etc.), sometimes nothing can alleviate anxiety in Triskaidekaphobiacs: it is not customary for there to be 13 steps up to the gallows, for example. But even though there are not 13 steps to the gallows, there remains the belief that there is by Triskaidekaphobiacs.

Indeed, sometimes, mere coincidence reinforces the anxiety of Triskaidekaphobiacs: that the Knights Templar were arrested on a Friday the 13th in the year 1307 might seem meaningless, but to a Triskaidekaphobiac, this seems significant. It is difficult to soothe such an irrational fear: facts that support the fear are accepted, and facts that challenge the fear are rejected.

The arrest and execution of Knights Templar

Friggatriskaidekaphobia
HMS Friday

Some people are also afraid of Fridays. And you can imagine that Friday the 13th has become a cause for irrational fear as well: this irrational fear is called Friggatriskaidekaphobia.

The story goes that at one time, the British Admiralty had a superstition to never launch a ship on a Friday. They decided to debunk this myth, so they decided to build a new ship. The keel was laid on a Friday, it was commissioned the HMS FRIDAY, crew was commissioned on a Friday, it set sail on a Friday…and was never heard from again.

But in fact, there has never been any Royal Navy ship of that name – though the story nevertheless is believed by those who fear Friday and 13.

The HMS Sutherland, a Type 23 Frigate

Monday

Some people look forward to Friday – because it is the beginning of a weekend rest. These people might dread Mondays, instead.

In the United Kingdom, more people commit suicide in England and Wales on Mondays than other days of the week; more people in the country in general call in sick; and more people worldwide surf the web.

But sometimes Monday is a happy occasion: the Church of Jesus Christ of Latter-day Saints spend one evening per week called Family Home Evening (FHE) or Family Night. This is usually Monday: families are encouraged to spend together in study, prayer and other family activities, and it becomes a kind of holiday.

Is there a day of the week that you dread? Or that you are even afraid of? Do you act differently on some days?

"Monday morning in New York City" (1907) Monday is a popular day to wash laundry dirtied from the previous week, and weekend

A 13 rayed star, presented as a relaxation recreational activity for adults or children: tracing or coloring in these sorts of geometric designs (whether oriented around 13 or not) can actually reduce anxiety

Beyond Fear
Mathematics of 13

When fear is set aside, 13 can be studied mathematically. 13 is not an especially special number, after all.

It is the third number in the second set of 10 (using base-10 numbering systems): in some other numbering systems, 13 doesn't even exist. For example, in binary, you'd count the same sum as 1101.

It is the 6th Prime Number (Prime Numbers are those which can only be wholly divided by themselves and 1): 2, 3, 5, 7 and 11 precede 13, and 17, 19, 23, 29, 31, 37 and many others follow it.

13 is the 7th Fibonacci number (Fibonacci numbers are those which are calculated by adding every two previous numbers in succession: 1+1 = 2, 2+1 = 3, 3+2 = 5, 5+3 = 8, 8+5 = 13.

With a standard 13-month lunar calendar, a 13th month in many lunar cultures represents a leap-month to keep the lunar and solar calendars in synchronization. But, in other calendar systems that are neither lunar nor solar, such as that 19 month system used by the Baha'I, or the 10 month Napoleonic calendar, or the 12 month Julian calendar most typically used today to approximate stellar rotational cycles, there is either no 13th month the 13th month is merely one among so many others.

Venus signifies "Friday" to many cultures – yet means something completely different to others...leaving aside any irrational fear of the day for a moment, what does Friday mean to you?

Friday

Similarly, Friday, when fear is set aside, is merely interesting: most cultures simply number days of the week instead of naming them (1ˢᵗ day, 2ⁿᵈ day, 3ʳᵈ day…) and in cultures which name days of weeks, most do not call that day "Friday," but have named it after their own traditional gods, reflecting ancient religious traditions associated with that day of the week – or after planets, which typically bore special significance to many early civilizations. This is typical in India (Shukravara) and Japan (Kinyobi), where the day is named after the planet Venus.

Similarly, in Arabic, the day is referred to as "al-jum'ah" which signifies the religious gathering that takes place on that day: in Greek, a similar term of Paraskevi (Παρασκευή) is used to describe the religious preparations typically made that day for the upcoming Sabbath celebration.

But not every culture divides time in terms of "weeks," and days are merely numbered into months and years.

And, in Thailand, and other nations where there has been a long tradition of multiculturalism, or many modern international offices, combinations of day-numbers, day-names (in Thailand, "wan suk" is named after Venus), pictograms, combined lunar/solar month (non-weekly) enumeration, notation on day/night changes to counts, and even color coding help people navigate the special significance each day means to their neighbors at a glance.

Overcoming Fear
Look at All the Facts

An old superstition says that if you have 13 letters in your name, you've got the devil's luck. It may sound stupid, but Charles Manson, Jack the Ripper, Jeffrey Dammer, Theodore Bundy and Albert De Salvo all have 13 letters.

…That is, if you disregard middle names.

The irrationality of Triskaidekaphobia – and all fear - is reinforced by accepting only information that supports the irrational fear, and disregarding information that contradicts it.

On Friday, October 13th, 1972, Uruguyan Air Force Flight 571 crashed in the Andes, killing 29 people. That exact same day, 174 people were killed when a Soviet Aeroflot crashed in a lake about half a mile from the runway.

Apollo 13 is the only unsuccessful moon mission so far. An oxygen tank exploded and the survival of the astronauts was really up in the air (no pun intended) for days until they all came home safely.

Of course, travel on the 13th, or even Friday the 13th is not statistically significantly more dangerous than flying any other day of the year. And plenty of other NASA missions with the number 13 designation were very successful. But a Triskaidekaphobiac would disregard the information that contradicts their irrational belief.

Bad luck, it seems, is seen only in selective facts.

The NASA shuttle orbiter mission STS-51-L of the Space Shuttle Challenger's 10th flight has no number 13, but was a failure – and the 13th mission was both successful and unremarkable

STS-13 was renamed mission STS-41c: the 13th mission of the Space Shuttle was also landed on Friday the 13th! The reason for the renaming was to accommodate NASA Administrator James M. Beggs's both Triskaidekaphobia and Friggatriskaidekaphobia... nevertheless, the crew had some good fun at the Administrator's expense by adopting the "black cat on a black cloud" patch for their mission (black cats are similarly regarded with superstitious fear: Ailurophobia; black clouds reference a fear of weather: Astraphobia) and keeping the number 13 on the patch... the mission was successful, and largely unremarkable.

Lucky Number

In some cultures, especially among some Cantonese-speaking areas, 13 is lucky – perhaps because it sounds like "sure to live" (14 is unlucky there – as it sounds like "sure to die.")

Colgate University was founded by 13 men, with $13 and 13 prayers – and there, 13 is very auspicious: Friday the 13th is the luckiest day of the year at Colgate University.

And in sports, many players will wear the number 13 for good luck: in 1966, Portugal achieved their best-ever result at the World Cup final tournaments by finishing third, thanks to a Mozambican-born striker, Eusebio, who has scored nine goals at World Cup — four of them in a 5-3 quarterfinal win over North Korea — and won the Golden Boot award as the tournament's top scorer while wearing the number 13. In the 1954 and 1974 World Cup finals, Germany's Max Morlock and Gerd Müller, respectively, played and scored in the final, wearing the number 13.

Jewish male children come of age in their 13th year.

On the United States of America's Flag, there are 13 stripes, and in the seal of the United States of America, the Eagle clutches 13 arrows, and an olive branch with 13 leaves, a shield with 13 stars. These are seen as good signs. If you're American. Not so much if you're British.

"King" Eusébio da Silva Ferreira

Some people have an irrational fear of spiders – while others will keep them as beloved pets. Some people keep snakes as pets – or climb mountains and work cleaning exterior windows of skyscrapers. There is nothing in this world that "everyone" is afraid of – or that "no one" is afraid of. Fear is very personal.

What are you afraid of? Does your fear prevent you from accomplishing your goals, or interfere with your day to day life? Is it debilitating? How have you, in the past, overcome your fears and changed the way you interact with what made you afraid?

Phobias – Nothing to Laugh At

Irrational fears are no laughing matter – and can be disabling diseases because of the anxiety they produce. Some people are afraid of the number 13, others have fears of the dark, or of snakes, bugs, heights – or even have social anxieties, or testing anxieties.

Irrational fears have many causes. Sometimes, genetics are involved, and sometimes physical, emotional or even psychological trauma. They can be caused by conditioning, and experience. Some fears result from philosophical concerns, or even spiritual ones.

Sometimes irrational fears are useful, and taught to children from a young age to keep them safe. Have you ever been told to be afraid of something?

When these irrational fears begin to interfere with normal life, or become debilitating, or incapacitating, the person suffering from them may seek the help of a psychologist, psychiatrist or personal physician. But no one is ever free from fear.

And it is so easy to feel unlucky.

Fearless

Fear is a natural and useful emotion – necessary to normal life and functioning. Have you ever benefited from a fear before?

But like any thought or feeling, you cannot let it control you.

People recover from phobia not when they become fearless, but when their fears no longer prevent them from living a normal life, no longer are incapacitating, no longer preventing them from achieving their needs and wants.

No one is fearless: fear is a natural result of thinking – as is all emotion. Without fear, or other emotions, a person can become just as dysfunctional as someone with too much fear, or irrational fear.

Other emotions, if experienced in excess or insufficiently can cause just as many problems as fear. Depression is another common ailment associated with too much of one emotion. But a person who has insufficient quantities of emotion, whose emotions are "muted," is equally ill.

Do you control your emotions – or do they control you? Are you comfortable feeling your emotions, confident that you won't act on them unless you need to or want to? Can you feel them, without acting on them?

The Most Common Fears

Fears of 13 and Friday are very rare, but phobia itself is relatively common – in some form or another. More than 10% people have a phobia which interferes with their life. More than 70% of people have a more mild form of phobia which does not interfere with their life.

Some theories suggest there is a genetic link to specific phobias as a kind of dormant survival mechanism: transmitted from parent to child for generations of humanity, and before the first human evolved, these instinctual responses once served a valuable purpose to our ancestors. Thus, all phobias are associated with more basic instincts of preserving life/avoiding death, and procreation – among others.

The most common phobias are social phobias: they can be so severe that they are considered an anxiety disorder and include excessive self-consciousness in social situations. Sometimes they are generalized, but sometimes they are specific, like being afraid of eating in the presence of others. 5% of people have a social phobia.

Agoraphobia is more than a fear of open spaces – when not generalized, it can become a specific fear of a particular place: a graveyard, a hospital, one or another kind of building, a public square, a particular store, etc. Yet while some people are afraid of one place, others are not. Some people even live and work in the places that others are afraid of! Do some places make you nervous?

Acrophobia is a fear of heights, but is also associated with a medical condition known as vertigo: the brain's inability to properly process depth of field perceived by the eye can result in discomfort, even pain, or dizziness, or other physical dysfunction – which the person becomes afraid of. However, while some are afraid of heights, others seek heights recreationally, in climbing.

Pteromehanophobia is a fear of flying – and can also be specific to a particular means of flying, such as aircraft. Yet as terrifying as a fear of flying is to some, others find it recreationally enjoyable, or even fly frequently as required by their profession.

Claustrophobia is more than a fear of enclosed spaces, but sometimes confinement, or even entrapment. Yet, while some people are afraid of confinement, others find it comforting.

Entomophobia is a fear of insects, whether generally, or specific to a fear of being bitten, or crawled on, or diseased. Bear in mind, some people are terrified of insects – while others keep them as pets. Or raise them commercially for agriculture (honey, meat, silk, etc.), medicine, science or hobby interest.

Ophidiophobia is a fear of snakes, whether generalized, or specific to being bitten, or strangled. But while some people are terrified of snakes, others keep them as pets, or raise them for medical, scientific, agricultural or hobby interest.

Cynophobia is a fear of dogs, whether specifically of being bitten or chased, or generally. Some people who are allergic to dogs develop a fear of dogs because they are afraid of the asthma or allergic reaction those dogs produce in them. Yet, others keep dogs as pets, raise them for food, or work alongside them in a variety of activities. Including activities where the dogs are trained to take advantage of this common fear and frighten people to protect property or persons.

Astraphobia is a fear of storms. Beyond the normal rush that booming thunder, wind, rain, heat, snow, or other weather produces, there are some who are deeply unsettled by any change in the weather, or by specific kinds of weather – or even by specific phenomenon of kinds of weather, like lightning, or flooding.

Trypanophobia is a fear of needles, but can be generalized into being cut, or probed, bleeding, having blood drawn, or even develop into fears of doctors or medical treatments.

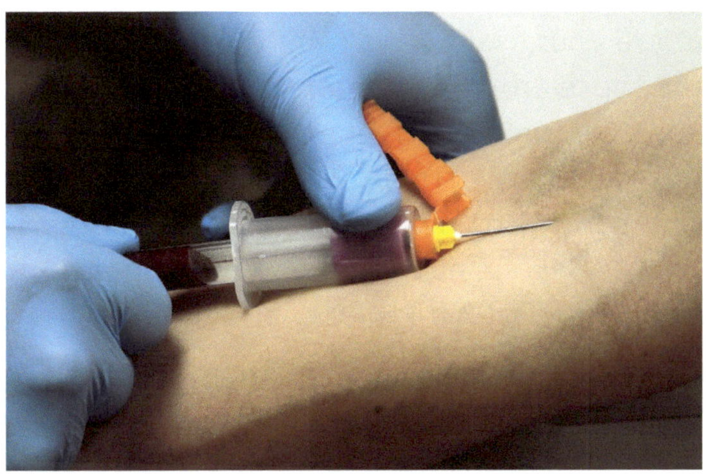

Treatment

People with phobias often realize their fear is irrational, but they're unable to do anything about it without help. And frequently, there is a phobia, an irrational fear, of seeking help associated with social anxiety! Even when fears can interfere with work, school, and personal relationships, someone might not be able to overcome their fear of asking for help to get treatment, or succeed in treatment.

Those suffering from phobia rely on the support and love of their family, friends and society – not only to understand it is ok to get help, but also in their recovery.

Phobia is treatable by modern medicine. Treatment for phobias can involve therapeutic techniques, medications, mental training or a combination of these.

So the next time you see a "missing floor," or "missing terminal" it might still seem silly to you – but remember, the compassion which motivates this sort of sensitivity is nevertheless admirable.

What are your friends and family afraid of? How can you make those around you more comfortable as they face – and eventually conquer - their fears? How can they make you more comfortable as you face and conquer your fears? How can you help them face their fears?

Do you, or anyone else you know, need help?

How can you best help them – and how can they best help you?

12
10
8
6
4
2
B
14
11
9
7
5
3
1
OPEN DOOR
OFF INS.
CAR TOP